The Word & Song

Christmas Storybook

A Celebration of God's Gift of Love

Stephen Elkins
AUTHOR

Tim O'Connor
ILLUSTRATOR

BROADMAN
& HOLMAN
PUBLISHERS

NASHVILLE, TENNESSEE

I t was Christmas Eve and the house was silent and still. A beautiful Christmas tree stood tall in front of the snow-drifted windows.

Shining through the frosty panes was the silvery moonlight, settling gently on the gifts, decorated in ribbons and bows. And in the quiet of that moment, high upon the mantle sat the most special decoration of all: the nativity scene.

And resting in the manger was the baby Jesus, God's special gift of love.   For He is the Promised One the prophets spoke of so many years before. His story is one of love, peace, and salvation.

God placed a beautiful star in the eastern sky as if to say, "Come and see the King ... He is born this day."

This is the story of God's wonderful Gift of Love.

Now in the days when Herod was King of Judea, there lived a priest named Zacharias. He had a wife named Elizabeth. They had grown old together but had no children.

One day Zacharias was in the temple preparing an offering to the Lord when suddenly, an angel appeared before him.

Zacharias was afraid! Then he heard the angel say, "Do not be afraid, for God has heard your prayers. Soon you and Elizabeth will have a little baby boy. You are to name him John, for he will be great in the kingdom of God. Because of his preaching many will repent and turn to the Lord. He will prepare the way for the coming Messiah."

Zacharias said to the angel, "How can this be true? I am too old to have children and so is my wife."

"I am Gabriel, a messenger sent by God to tell you this wonderful news. But since you have not believed me, you shall be unable to speak until all of these things have happened." Then, as quickly as he had come, Gabriel disappeared.

Outside the temple, the people were waiting for Zacharias.

Finally he came out, unable to speak. He used sign language to try to tell them what had happened.

They thought he had seen a vision!

Finally, a silent Zacharias returned home. Soon Elizabeth discovered that she was going to have a baby, just as Gabriel had said.

Now sometime later, the angel Gabriel was sent by God to the city of Nazareth to visit a young woman named Mary. She was engaged to marry a carpenter named Joseph.

But before their wedding day, Gabriel came to her and said, "Hello favored one, the Lord is with you!" Mary had never heard such a greeting before and wondered, "What does this mean?"

Gabriel spoke again, "Do not be afraid Mary, for I have a message for you from the Lord.

You are going to have a baby boy and you shall call His name Jesus. He will be great and will be called the Son of God, and His kingdom will have no end." Mary was confused. "How can this be?" she asked. "I have no husband yet."

Gabriel answered, "Nothing is impossible with God. Even Elizabeth your relative is going to have a baby, though she is very old. Nothing is impossible with God."

"I am a servant of the Lord," said Mary. "Let all that you have said be done in my life." And in an instant, the angel was gone.

Mary couldn't wait to tell Elizabeth about Gabriel's visit. She left Nazareth at once. When she arrived at Zacharias' house, she called, "Elizabeth! It is me, Mary." When Elizabeth heard Mary's voice, her baby jumped inside her and the Spirit of God filled her.

Elizabeth embraced Mary and said, "Blessed are you among women Mary, and blessed is the little baby inside you.

I am so very happy that the mother of my Lord has come to see me!"

Mary wondered, "How could Elizabeth know about the baby Jesus? I haven't told her yet." But Mary said, "I am so happy because God is my Lord and Savior. Holy is His name."

Then Mary prayed, "I will praise the
name of the Lord forever,
I will rejoice in my
God and Savior.

The Lord will be
merciful to me
and to all
His children.
I shall love Him
with all my
heart."

13

Mary stayed with Elizabeth and Zacharias for three months. Soon it was time for Elizabeth to have her baby.

Zacharias worked very hard getting everything ready for the arrival of his new son.

Elizabeth gave birth to a beautiful baby boy, just as the angel had said.

When their relatives and neighbors heard this good news, they came to celebrate the birth of the child.

"He's so beautiful," said a friend. "And he looks so strong! What are you going to name him?"

Their friends and church leaders expected his name to be Zacharias like his father's.

But Elizabeth said "No, his name will be John."

"You can't call him John," they said. "Let's ask Zacharias what the child's name will be."

On a tablet Zacharias wrote, "His name is John." At that very moment, Zacharias could once again speak. And oh, how he praised the Lord!

"This must be a very special child," the people said, "for the hand of the Lord is upon him."

Then Zacharias prayed this very special prayer:

"We bless You, O Lord, for we know You have given us this child to fulfill Your plans. For You will send a Savior soon. You have remembered Your promise to Abraham.

This, my child, will be a prophet who will prepare the way of the Lord.

You are a wonderful God and we will serve You."

Mary returned to her home in Nazareth. When she told Joseph all of the things that had happened to her and Elizabeth, he was very confused.

But one night as he slept, an angel of the Lord appeared to him in a dream and said, "Mary is a good woman. Do not put her away. Take her as your wife, for her baby is a miracle baby that God Himself has given her."

"And you shall call His name Jesus, for He will save His people from their sins."

When Joseph awoke from his dream, he did exactly what the angel asked him to do. He took Mary as his wife and he never doubted again.

Now it came about that the Roman king, Caesar Augustus, wanted to know how many people were living in his kingdom. So he ordered everyone, including Joseph and Mary, to return to their own city to be counted.

Caesar's order came at a very bad time, for Mary was ready to have her baby. But still she and Joseph made the journey from Nazareth to the city of David which is called Bethlehem.

The journey was very tiring and the evenings were very cold. They slept under the night sky beside the glowing firelight.

Joseph took care of Mary and God took care of them both.

Together Mary and Joseph traveled the rocky roads, up from Galilee from the City of Nazareth, to Judea to the city of David, which is called Bethlehem. This was Joseph's hometown.

The long, dusty trail had been very difficult for Mary, and the baby was coming soon.

When they arrived in Bethlehem, it was very crowded. Because of Caesar's order, travelers were flooding into the city to be counted and all the inns were full.

Mary was ready to have her baby. Joseph looked everywhere for a room, but there was none to be found.

Finally, Joseph met an innkeeper who pointed to the stable behind his inn. "You will find no room in this city tonight," he said. "You may rest in my stable. It will be dry and warm."

Up the hill went Mary, Joseph, and the little donkey. Finally, they came to the stable where they were greeted by sheep and livestock.

There, under the night sky amidst the cows and sheep, Jesus Christ, the Son of God, was born. Mary and Joseph loved Him so much.

Since Mary had no baby bed, she wrapped Jesus in swaddling clothes and laid Him in a manger, which is a feeding box for cows. There, under the stars of Bethlehem, the baby Jesus slept.

But the baby sleeping in the manger that night was more than a beautiful child. He was the promise of all the ages, the Living Word, God's very special gift to the world.

For He had been sent by God Himself as a precious gift of love to you and me.

Jesus would take away the sins of the world and give us the gift of eternal life.

Because of Jesus all the world can rejoice!

Nearby, there was a group of
shepherds keeping watch over their
flocks of sheep. It was late, and
they were making sure all the
little lambs were safe in the fold.

Suddenly, an angel of the
Lord appeared before them and
the darkness was filled with light!
The shepherds were so afraid!

"What could it be?" they thought.
For they had never seen
anything so wondrous!

Then the angel spoke. "Do not be afraid, for I bring you good news of a great joy!

Today in Bethlehem, your Savior is born who is Christ the Lord.

Come and see the Lord!"

"You will know it is Jesus when you find Him wrapped in swaddling clothes and lying in a manger."

Then suddenly, many angels appeared before them, praising God and saying, "Glory to God in the highest. And on earth, peace among men with whom He is pleased."

27

When the angels departed, the shepherds said, "Let's go to Bethlehem right now to see this thing that has happened."

So they hurried into town and found their way to the stable where Mary and Joseph watched over the baby Jesus.

And just as the angel had said, they found Jesus wrapped in swaddling clothes and lying in a manger.

Now when they had seen all this, they told everyone about Jesus and the appearance of angels.

The shepherds went back to their flocks, praising God all the way!

For they had seen the precious baby who is Christ the Lord.

O how their hearts were filled with joy and thanksgiving. The promised gift of all the ages had come at last!

Truly, it was a glorious night. All was calm and the stars overhead shown brightly, for Jesus Christ the Lord was born.

As Jesus lay asleep on the manger hay, Mary sat in wonder.

God had been so good to her and Joseph. He had made a way when it looked like there was no way.

But she knew God was a God of miracles and Jesus was the greatest miracle of all!

After Jesus was born, wise men from eastern countries arrived in Jerusalem saying, "Where is the child who has been born King of the Jews? For we have seen His star shining in the east and have come to worship Him."

Mary and Joseph welcomed the travelers who knelt before the Christ child. They beheld His glory and presented Him with gifts of gold, frankincense, and myrrh. They worshiped the One born King of the Jews.

Having spent time with their Messiah, the wise men left Bethlehem, overjoyed that they had found the king.

They waved goodbye to Mary and Joseph and began the long journey home.

And what became of baby John and baby Jesus?

Baby John grew up to become John the Baptist,
the one Jesus said was the greatest to ever live.
He would prepare the hearts of the people
to receive the kingdom of God.

The baby Jesus was born
Lord and Savior, the one
who would give His life
that we might one day
receive the gift of heaven.

What an amazing gift!
What an amazing story!

And there upon the mantle sits the nativity scene. Mary kneels while Joseph looks on in wonder. The shepherds gather 'round to praise the Lord Jesus while angels fill the skies with singing.

Yes, it is Christmas Eve, and the house is silent and still. The gifts await us under the Christmas tree. But always remember the greatest gift ever given was the precious gift of Jesus.

For God so loved the world that He gave His only begotten Son,

Jesus ...

the greatest gift of all!

The Word & Song Christmas Storybook was adapted from the original ***The Word & Song Bible.*** Seventeen of today's best-known Christian entertainers, authors, speakers, and leaders are featured on ***The Word & Song Bible.*** These include Larnelle Harris as the voice of the apostle Paul, Steve Green as the voice of Jesus, Max Lucado as the voice of John, Joni Eareckson Tada as the voice of Mary, Rebecca St. James, Reggie White, Twila Paris, Roy Clark, George Beverly Shea, Steve Camp, and others.

The entire line of Word and Song Products features:

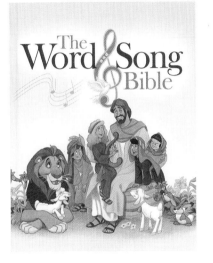

The Word & Song Bible
$19.99   0-8054-1689-7

The Word & Song Bible with CDs
$39.99   0-8054-1690-0

The Word & Song Bible CD Audio Pack
$24.99   0-8054-1692-7

The Word & Song Bible Cassette Audio Pack
$19.99   0-8054-1693-5

The Word & Song Bible with Cassettes
$34.99   0-8054-1691-9

The Word & Song Songbook, Vol 1 (Old Testament)
with Split-Track cassette
$12.99   0-8054-1694-3

The Word & Song Songbook, Vol 2 (New Testament)
with Split-Track cassette
$12.99   0-8054-1695-1